AN ALIEN ROBOT'S
COOKBOOK

AN ALIEN ROBOT'S COOKBOOK

Discover Real Recipes

RUTH FANKUSHEN KUNKEL

Illustrations by

**GABRIEL KUNKEL &
RUTH FANKUSHEN KUNKEL**

*Big thanks to Roger and Joey Kunkel, Deborah Madison, Liza Jernow, Bob
Hessen, Babz Bitela, Jill Stevenson, Janis Cooke for her mother's amazing beet
recipe, Aunt Judy and Uncle Herb, Kurt Polzin, Holly Istas for her wondrous
tofu triangle recipe, everyone ever connected to the Delta of Venus Café, and
especially to our neighbors at Muir Commons Co-Housing for tasting the
recipes. Tremendous thanks also go to our family members for their stellar
support.*

For our Friends
Near and Far

CONTENTS
(For your Table)

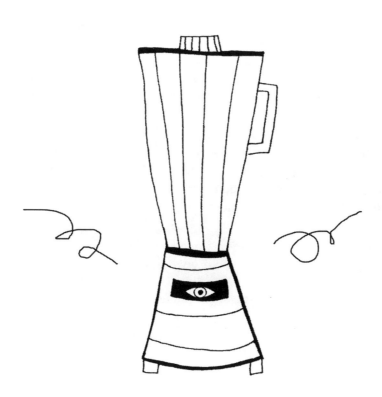

Introduction, Version 1
The Author's Story

An Alien Robot's Cookbook contains recipes that my sons like to eat and prepare.

This cookbook began as a journey to find something that my son Gabriel would eat besides pizza, hot dogs, and cereal. After some thought, he admitted that he enjoyed pumpkin muffins, sautéed zucchini, and nachos. Gradually, the list grew to include some favorite recipes from my former restaurant, the Delta of Venus Café. Eventually, Gabriel's list grew so long and became so valuable to me that I decided to put all of the recipes together in this book so that they would be easily available.

Aside from suggesting recipes, cooking the dishes with me, and taste-testing the results (with brother Joey and friends Noah and Teliz), Gabriel created 97% of the original artwork. I simply added details to his far-out sketches of aliens, robots, and other creatures.

That is *my* story of how an *Alien Robot's Cookbook* came into being.

However, there is another version…

Robot Cook #4U82

Introduction, Version 2
The Alien Robot's Story

Log Readout from Robot #4U82:

- Gather tragulas for supper. Enter borrowed craft to return home. Turn ignition. Major malfunction. Rocket into unfamiliar galaxy.

- Crash-land on solid surface. Coordinates indicate Planet Earth. Run diagnostics. Damage to self is minimal. Damage to space car is total. Irreparable.

- Host planet appears to be stable.

- Fleshy creature materializes in portal. It speaks. Switch on Translation Mechanism. The being intones, "Hello? Are you okay in there? Do you need help?"

- No response. Mechanism works slower than usual. Creature speaks again. "I am Gabriel," it says.

- I respond. "I am Cooking Robot #4U82."

- The Gabriel uses a tool to pry my unit out of crushed wreck. The Gabriel introduces me to two larger creatures like himself. "Mom" and "Dad." A smaller version of The Gabriel is also present. "This is Joey," says The Gabriel. Then The Gabriel introduces me to "Refrigerator," "Oven," "Stove," and "Dishwasher."

- I begin work. I cook Earth Dishes for The Gabriel's family. They smile. They repeatedly say, "Yum."

- On seventh day on Planet Earth, I receive communication through Toaster. Message indicates imminent arrival of rescue craft.

- While family restores energy through sleep, I print pages of recipes for The Gabriel to follow.

- I fasten pages together. I make a Book.

- I deposit Book in kitchen, next to Stove.

- I push "Potscrubber" button on Dishwasher. Molecules rearrange.

- I travel home.

Safety Notes & Guidelines

Cooking is easy and fun, especially when you follow the recipe's directions.

Knives are sharp. Ask an adult before using a knife.

Hot ovens and stoves can burn. Wear protective oven mitts or use insulated potholders whenever you reach into an oven or grab the handle of a cook pot.

Do not wear clothes with loose-fitting sleeves when you cook. A dangling sleeve could catch on fire.

Do not leave cooking food unattended.

If you become agitated or frustrated, please seek help before you go berserk.

BLAST OFF *for* BREAKFAST

Hard-Boiled Egg Orbs

People eat hard-boiled eggs on toast, in salad, or alone with a bit of salt. Each oval orb contains a surprise. Can you remove the shell in one piece? Don't give up. There's plenty of time to perfect your pursuits.

4 eggs (orbs)
Water

Gently place the orbs into a pot. Cover them with water. Boil. Turn off the heat. Cover the pot with a lid. Wait 10 minutes.

Remove the eggs carefully with a slotted spoon. Put them into a bowl filled with super-cold water.

Let the eggs cool before peeling and eating.

SERVES 4

LEVEL 1: EASY

Portal Toast

Warning! This toast and egg dish may transport you to another place. At the very least, it will provide you with a tasty breakfast. Prepare with (or without) cheese, pepper, and ketchup. By the way, portals are entrances or gateways.

1 slice bread
1 teaspoon butter
1 egg orb
1 tablespoon shredded cheese, optional
Salt and pepper

Remove the center of bread slice with a circular cookie cutter. Or you can use a drinking glass turned upside down. Remove the circle center and eat it.

Put the butter into a frying pan and heat it over a medium flame. Add the bread slice. Break your egg so that it lands inside the circular hole. (Sometimes it's easier to break the egg into a bowl first and to transfer the egg into the bread's hole.) Turn the heat to low. Cook for 3 minutes.

Using a spatula, turn over the egg-filled bread slice. Sprinkle the egg portion with cheese, if that sounds good to you. Cook for 3 minutes more over low heat until the egg appears to be done. Some kids enjoy this item with ketchup.

MAKES 1 SERVING

LEVEL 1: EASY

Universal Breakfast Burritos

These Mexican-inspired burritos include two kinds of cheese, cottage cheese and cheddar cheese. If you prefer, you can substitute ricotta for the cottage cheese and jack or mozzarella for the cheddar.

10 eggs
10 large flour tortillas
½ cup flour
Salsa
1 teaspoon baking powder
½ teaspoon salt
1 pint cottage cheese
3 cups shredded cheddar cheese
¼ cup melted butter

Preheat the oven to 350°F.

Beat the eggs in a bowl. Add the flour, baking powder, salt, shredded cheese, cottage cheese, and the melted butter. Blend well. Pour the mixture into a greased 9x13-inch baking dish. Bake for 35 minutes. Cool for 5 minutes, then cut into 10 equal-sized pieces.

Heat the tortillas in a microwave oven for 1 minute or put them in an ungreased frying pan to warm. Place a piece of the filling inside each tortilla and add a spoonful of salsa. Wrap up each tortilla and serve with salsa and guacamole, etc.

SERVES 10

LEVEL 2: LESS SIMPLE

16

Big Bang Breakfast Potatoes

These exceptional breakfast potatoes explode with even more flavor when topped with Supernova Salsa, Gravitational Guacamole, sour cream, or any type of cheese you fancy.

4 medium baking (russet) potatoes
2 tablespoons butter or vegetable oil
Optional: 1 onion, chopped and/or 1 green pepper, chopped
½ teaspoon salt
½ teaspoon paprika
Pepper

Scrub the potatoes well. You don't need to peel them, but chop them into bite-sized pieces. Place the potato cubes into a large pot, covered with cold water. Boil the potatoes for about 7 minutes, or until tender. Then drain the potatoes very, very carefully.

Heat the butter or oil in a heavy skillet (non-stick or cast-iron work best). Add the onions (if you are using them) and cook for about 2 minutes. Then add the green peppers. Continue to cook the vegetables for a couple of minutes, stirring occasionally.

Add the drained potatoes and cook over medium heat until they are crispy and brown all over. Shake on some paprika, salt, and pepper.

Add cheddar or jack cheese just before serving. Mix in the cheese to melt it.

SERVES 4

According to the Big Bang Theory, our universe started between 10 billion and 20 billion years ago with a gigantic explosion. The Big Bang Theory is widely accepted, but it has still never been proven.

LEVEL 2: LESS SIMPLE

Planetary Pecan Muffins

These nutty muffins have a crumbly texture, rather like biscuits. If you mix the batter too much, they will become too dry. Add a half cup of fresh, frozen, or dried fruit if you like. The bumpy tops of these muffins resemble the rough surfaces of many planets. Hold one in your hand and think about space.

¾ cup chopped pecans
3 tablespoons butter
3 tablespoons honey
1 cup rolled oats
1½ cups flour
½ teaspoon baking soda
1½ teaspoons baking powder
¼ teaspoon salt
1 cup buttermilk
1 egg
¼ teaspoon vanilla
Optional: Pieces of fruit

Preheat the oven to 375°F.

Toast the pecans and oats in a skillet over low heat for 10 minutes. Watch them so that they don't burn. (Nuts burn quickly). Melt the butter and honey together in a separate pot or in the microwave.

In another bowl, sift together the flour, soda, powder and salt. Stir in the pecans and oats. Make a crater in the center of the dry ingredients. In a separate bowl, beat together the wet ingredients (including the butter and honey). Pour this wet mixture into the hole. Mix just enough to blend everything. Fold in fruit, if using. Pour batter into greased muffin tins (or paper muffin cups) and bake for about 23 minutes.

MAKES 12

LEVEL 2: LESS SIMPLE

Pumpkin Muffins

Sprinkle walnuts on top of these moist muffins to add texture, interest, and crunch.

1½ cups flour
1 teaspoon baking soda
½ teaspoon baking powder
¾ teaspoon salt
½ teaspoon nutmeg
½ teaspoon cinnamon
1½ cups sugar
½ cup vegetable oil
2 eggs
1 cup canned pumpkin
1/3 cup water
Optional: walnuts, chopped

Preheat the oven to 350°F.

Mix the dry ingredients together in a large bowl. Stir in the oil, eggs, and pumpkin. Using an electric mixer on low speed, add the water slowly until everything is well blended (or you could stir by hand).

Pour the batter into greased muffin tins, or into paper muffin cups. Sprinkle the muffin tops with chopped walnuts, if desired. Bake for 23 minutes.

MAKES 12 MUFFFINS

LEVEL 1: EASY

19

Astral Apple Muffins

These sweet muffins are stellar. You could substitute persimmons for the apples, and they would still shine brightly. Another day, you could try substituting peaches. Do you dare?

4 cups Granny Smith apples, peeled and chopped
1 cup sugar
2 eggs
½ cup vegetable oil
2 teaspoons vanilla
2 teaspoons lemon juice
2 cups flour
1 teaspoon cinnamon
2 teaspoons baking soda
1 teaspoon nutmeg
1 teaspoon salt
1 cup raisins

Preheat the oven to 350°F.

Mix the apples and sugar together in a large bowl. Set aside.

In another bowl, combine the eggs, oil, vanilla, and lemon juice. Stir until no lumps remain. Add this mixture to the apples and sugar. Add the flour, cinnamon, baking soda, nutmeg, and salt. Mix until combined, but do not over-mix.

Stir in the raisins. Pour the batter into greased muffin tins or paper muffin cups. Bake for 23-25 minutes.

MAKES 18 MUFFINS

LEVEL 2: LESS SIMPLE

Supersonic Scones

Some kids like these scones with chocolate chips, raisins, or dried apricots. Any way you make them, they'll soon vanish.

2 cups flour
1 teaspoon cream of tartar
½ teaspoon baking soda
½ teaspoon salt
1-2 tablespoons sugar
4 tablespoons unsalted butter, chilled and cut into small pieces
¾ cup milk
Optional: ½ cup chocolate chips or ½ cup raisins or chopped, dried apricots

Preheat oven to 450°F.

Whisk flour, cream of tartar, baking soda, salt and sugar together in large bowl. Use your clean fingers to mix the butter into the flour mixture until the mixture resembles coarse meal.

Make a hole or crater in the middle of mixture and pour the milk into it. Work quickly. Blend the ingredients with a rubber spatula or wooden spoon. Over-mixing may make your scones tough.

Make a dough ball. Pat the ball down to 1/2-inch thickness. Cut the dough into 8 equal-sized triangular pieces. Put the separate pieces onto a greased baking sheet, separated by at least 1 inch. Bake for 11 minutes.

MAKES 8

* The phrase "supersonic" is used to define a speed that is beyond the speed of sound. Speeds greater than 5 times the speed of sound are often referred to as "hypersonic." The speed of sound is 770 miles per hour.

LEVEL 2: LESS SIMPLE

Black Hole Banana Bread

This moist banana bread can be made with fresh or frozen bananas, with chocolate chips, or without them. Try carob chips sometime. They work well, too.

½ cup butter (one stick)
¾ cup sugar
2 eggs, beaten
3 ripe bananas, mashed
2 cups flour
1 teaspoon baking soda
½ teaspoon salt
1 teaspoon vanilla
½ cup chopped walnuts
½ cup chocolate chips

Preheat the oven to 350°F.

Cream the butter and sugar and mix until fluffy. Add the eggs one at a time. Beat well after each one. Sift the flour, baking soda, and salt together. Add this dry mixture to the batter. Add the mashed bananas, vanilla, walnuts, and the chocolate chips.

Pour into a greased loaf pan. Bake for 55 minutes. Cool for 10 minutes. Slice and enjoy before it disappears!

MAKES 1 LOAF

* A black hole's gravitational field is so strong that almost nothing can escape its pull. Even light cannot escape. As a result, a black hole's interior is dark. Black holes differ in size.

LEVEL 2: LESS SIMPLE

Blue Sky Blueberry Bread

Bring this blueberry bread on a picnic. The ants will thank you.

1/3 cup margarine or butter, at room temperature
¾ cup sugar
2 eggs, beaten
1 cup buttermilk
2 cups flour
½ teaspoon baking soda
½ teaspoon baking powder
½ teaspoon salt
½ cup blueberries, fresh or frozen

Preheat the oven to 350°F.

Beat the margarine (or butter) and sugar until fluffy. Add the eggs and the buttermilk. Mix well.

Combine the flour, baking soda, baking powder, and salt. Add to the margarine mixture. Fold in the blueberries until just blended. Do not over mix.

Pour the mixture into a greased loaf pan. Bake for 45 minutes. Insert a toothpick into the center of the bread. If the toothpick emerges clean, then your blueberry bread is done. If not, then bake the bread for an additional few minutes and check it again.

MAKES 1 LOAF

Why is the sky blue? Simply put, the white light from the sun is a mixture of all colors of the rainbow. Blue color is scattered more easily than the others

LEVEL 1: EASY

Mission Control Cornbread

Soften butter and mix it with honey. The sweet butter enhances this hearty cornbread at breakfast, lunch, or dinner. If you feel very adventurous, you could chop ½ teaspoon of rosemary and toss it into the batter for an herb-filled sensation.

1½ cups cornmeal
2½ cups milk
2 cups flour
1 teaspoon baking powder
1 teaspoon salt
2/3 cup white sugar
2 eggs
½ cup vegetable oil

Preheat the oven to 400°F.

In small bowl, combine the cornmeal with the milk. Let stand for 5 minutes. In a large bowl, whisk together the flour, baking powder, salt, and the sugar. Mix this together with the cornmeal mixture. Add the eggs and the oil. Blend until no lumps remain.

Pour the batter into a greased pie pan, (or spread the batter over a pie pan full of chili to make Tamale Pie). Bake for approximately 30 minutes. Cornbread should appear golden on top.

SERVES 4-6

The main job of Mission Control is to supervise space assignments using radios and other forms of communication. The center manages all the stages of the space journey from the point of liftoff until the end of the mission.

LEVEL 1: EASY

Routine Robocakes from the Pancake Galaxy

You can also make waffles using this recipe if you reduce the amount of buttermilk to ¾ cup and don't use the baking powder.

1 cup flour
2 tablespoons sugar
1 teaspoon baking powder
½ teaspoon baking soda
¼ teaspoon salt
1 cup buttermilk
1 tablespoon vegetable oil
1 egg, beaten

Greetings From the Pancake Galaxy!

In a mixing bowl, combine the flour, sugar, baking powder, baking soda and salt. Stir until blended. Make a crater in the center of the ingredients.

In another bowl, combine the buttermilk, oil and the beaten egg. Add these wet ingredients into the middle of the dry ingredients. Stir until blended again, but not much more than that.

Lightly oil a griddle or frying pan. Once the pan is hot, pour the batter into small pancakes. Flip when bubbles appear and the edges look cooked. Serve with butter and syrup. To freeze, wrap first in foil.

SERVES 2-4

The Pancake Galaxy is real: it's a polar ring galaxy in the constellation Ursa Major. It has a set of odd swirls going around the center of a mostly normal galaxy. The Pancake Galaxy was once called the "most unusual galaxy." It is also called the Helix Galaxy.

LEVEL 1: EASY

Apple Robocakes

This recipe earns a LEVEL 3: CHALLENGING classification because it requires separating eggs. Make your robocakes with applesauce for a plainer robocake or use chunks of apple for a more textured treat.

2 eggs, separated
1 cup of applesauce (pg. 85) or chopped, peeled apples
1 cup of flour, sifted
1 tablespoon of sugar
1½ teaspoons of melted butter
1½ teaspoons of baking powder
½ teaspoon of salt
¼ teaspoon of cinnamon
¼ teaspoon of vanilla
Cooking oil

Sift the flour, salt, and baking powder into a mixing bowl. Add all of the other ingredients, except for the eggs and butter.

To separate eggs: Carefully crack each egg over a small bowl. Let the white parts slip into the bowl while keeping the yellow yolks inside the shells. Now put the yolks into a different bowl.

Beat the egg yolks. Add the melted butter to the yolks. Add this mixture to the other batter. Now beat the egg whites in a separate bowl until stiff (help may be necessary at this point, either from an adult or an electric mixer. Your best help may come in the form of an adult *with* an electric mixer).

Fold the stiff egg whites into the batter. Heat a spoonful of oil in a skillet and ladle in the batter to make robocakes. When bubbles appear, flip the cakes once. Cook until done (about 3 minutes per side). SERVES 2-4

LEVEL 3: CHALLENGING

Banana-Walnut Robocakes

When did bananas and walnuts first meet each other? And what could create a more perfect combination? How about whipped cream on top?

1 egg
1 cup buttermilk
2 tablespoons cooking oil
1 cup flour
1 tablespoon sugar
1 teaspoon baking powder
½ teaspoon soda
½ teaspoon salt
½ teaspoon vanilla extract
1 ripe banana, mashed
½ cup walnuts, chopped

Beat the egg (but not to a pulp). Add the remaining ingredients in the order listed above (except for the walnuts). Beat together until smooth. Grease and heat the frying pan or griddle. Ladle batter by 1/4 cupful into the pan.

Flip the robocakes when bubbles appear. Bake the other side until golden, about 3 minutes. Serve with butter and maple syrup. Garnish with chopped walnuts.

SERVES 2-4

LEVEL 2: LESS SIMPLE

Crispy Potato Robocakes

Robocakes are not just for breakfast anymore. Within the Jewish tradition, these robocakes are called *latkes*, and they stand as the irresistible centerpiece of the Hanukkah meal. On Earth, you will find that potato pancakes can be made any number of ways. You could grate the potatoes, or mash them first. This recipe is very simple and can be very relaxing to prepare.

6 medium potatoes, cubed (you don't need to peel them, but please scrub!)
1 small onion, grated
2 tablespoons flour
2 eggs, beaten
1 1/2 teaspoons salt
2 tablespoons chopped parsley

Using a kitchen blender, combine the eggs, salt, parsley, onion, and half of the potatoes. Add the flour and the remaining potatoes. Blend again.

Heat the butter or oil in a frying pan. Pour in the batter and fry until crisp. Turn each robocake halfway through the cooking process. When done, place on a paper towel to absorb the excess oil. Serve these crispy potato robocakes with Adaptable Applesauce (pg. 85) and sour cream.

SERVES 4

LEVEL 2: LESS SIMPLE

Earth Crunch Granola

This granola is sweet, nutty, and satisfying. Try it. Share it. Granola makes a good gift when presented in a clean container along with a bow.

3 cups rolled oats
1 cup bran
½ cup almonds, chopped
½ cup walnuts, chopped
1 cup shredded coconut
½ cup nonfat dry milk
¾ cup honey
¼ cup vegetable oil
½ cup water
1 cup raisins or dried cranberries, or dried cherries

Preheat the oven to 250°F.

In a large mixing bowl, combine the oats, bran, nuts, coconut and milk powder. In another bowl, combine the honey, oil, and water. Gradually add the liquid ingredients to the dry ingredients. Mix well. Spread mixture onto cookie sheet.

Bake for 45 minutes total, but stir the granola every 15 minutes. (Remember to wear your protective oven mitts!) Remove the pan from the oven and pour into a large bowl. Allow granola to cool, and then stir in the raisins.

MAKES 9 CUPS

* Once in awhile, people do eat clay or dirt, perhaps as part of a religious ceremony, or to help cure a disease. Eating dirt can satisfy certain nutritional needs. (However, we suggest that you eat this granola if you ever get the urge to eat soil. The granola tastes better and your dentist will not complain.)

LEVEL 1: EASY

Overnight French Toast

This French toast works while you sleep. Serve with orange wedges for a complete meal.

4 eggs
2/3 cup orange juice
1/3 cup milk
¼ cup white sugar
¼ teaspoon nutmeg
¼ teaspoon vanilla extract
½ loaf bread, cut into slices
1/3 cup butter, melted
½ cup chopped pecans

In a large bowl, beat the eggs with the orange juice, milk, sugar, nutmeg and vanilla. Place the bread slices in a tightly spaced single layer in the bottom of a flat dish or baking pan. Pour the milk mixture over the bread slices. Cover the pan with foil or plastic wrap, and refrigerate overnight. If you can do so, turn the bread slices over in the middle of the night. Otherwise, do this step before you go to sleep.

In the morning, preheat the oven to 350°F.

Spread the melted butter evenly into the bottom of another baking dish. Arrange the wet bread slices in a single layer within the pan. Sprinkle on the pecans. Bake until golden, about 23 minutes. Be careful not to burn this delectable dish. Check baking progress regularly, especially toward the end of the baking time.

SERVES 4

* Night happens because the earth is always turning, and the part of the earth that is turned away from the sun and in its shadow is called "night."*

LEVEL 2: LESS SIMPLE

31

Four Celestial Spreads

Apply these heavenly spreads atop bagels, crackers, bread, and more. Store them in airtight containers in the refrigerator.

Dill Spread

1 (8 oz.) package cream cheese, softened
¼ cup milk or cream
1 teaspoon dried or 1 tablespoon fresh dill
½ Onion, Optional

Pulse the onion in a food processor, and then add the other ingredients.

Ricotta-Pesto Spread

2 cups Ricotta cheese
2 tablespoons Positively-Charged Pesto
1 tablespoon Parmesan cheese, grated
Salt and Pepper

Mix everything together. Add this ricotta-pesto mixture to your favorite cooked pasta, or simply try it on a toasted bagel.

Pineapple Cream Cheese Spread

1 (8 oz.) package cream cheese, softened
1 tablespoon apricot jam
½ cup crushed pineapple
2 teaspoons honey
Optional: 1/3 cup coconut flakes

Blend the cream cheese, jam, crushed pineapple, and honey. Add the coconut flakes if you like, and mix well.

Cinnamon-Sugar Cream Cheese Spread

1 (8 oz.) package cream cheese, softened
2/3 cup brown or white sugar
1¼ teaspoons cinnamon
Optional: raisins, chopped walnuts, chocolate chips, chopped dried fruit

Combine the cream cheese with the brown sugar and cinnamon. Stir in 1 or 2 tablespoons of the optional ingredients, if you like. Mix thoroughly.

* A celestial sphere is an imaginary ball around the Earth onto which the Sun, Moon, stars, and planets seem to come into view.

LEVEL 1: EASY

A Brainy Burst of Breakfast Ideas

Feeling tired? Try one of these breakfast ideas. You'll revive in no time.

1. Toast a bagel or a slice of wheat bread. Spread with cream cheese. Top with alfalfa sprouts.

2. Toast a bagel or an English muffin. Spread with peanut butter. Top with banana or apple slices. Add honey if desired.

3. Split a baguette lengthwise. Spread each half with cream cheese and top with pesto. Add softened sun-dried tomato pieces. (Or you could use a bagel, or a slice of bread in place of the baguette).

4. Make a serving of quick-style oatmeal (regular oatmeal is even better). Add butter, milk, maple syrup, and cinnamon. Top with raisins, if desired.

5. Get yourself a bowl of cereal. Earth Crunch Granola is good. Pour on some milk or soymilk. Add a few pieces of fresh fruit.

6. Beat two eggs in a bowl. Add a bit of water or milk to the eggs. Heat 1 tablespoon of butter in a frying pan. Turn the heat to medium-low and pour the eggs into the pan. Stir frequently to scramble the eggs. Once the eggs begin to cook, add a few pinches of shredded cheese. Eat with ketchup.

7. Put some plain yogurt into a small bowl. Sprinkle the yogurt with Earth Crunch Granola and add a teaspoon of honey. Top with sliced strawberries, peaches, or blueberries. (If you are using flavored yogurt, omit the honey.)

LEVEL 1: EASY

Alien Green Beans

Do not be afraid. These green beans come in peace. But seriously folks, these vegetables taste so fresh and glorious that you may want to branch out and substitute asparagus or chard for the green beans at another meal.

1½ pounds green beans
2 tablespoons butter
Salt and pepper

Remove each green bean end. Cut the green bean into 2-3 segments. Carefully drop the pieces into a pot of boiling water. Add 1 teaspoon of salt to the water, too. Cook uncovered for about 6 minutes. (If you cover the pot, the beans may turn gray, and gray beans are not attractive.)

Drain the beans in a colander (a bowl with holes). Rinse under cold water. Dry the beans (either put them into a clean kitchen towel or shake them well). Toss the dry, warm beans with butter. Add salt, and pepper too, if that is your preference.

SERVES 4 TO 6 EARTHLINGS

LEVEL 1: EASY

Bumble Beets

Behold the beet. Eaten alone, the beet tastes great. When paired with the bee's golden honey, the beet sweetens even more. Close your eyes, take a bite, and listen.

SUGGESTION: Serve beets atop a bed of steamed spinach for a complementary color and taste sensation.

3 cups beets
1/3 cup honey
1 tablespoon cornstarch
½ cup red wine vinegar
5 whole cloves
Salt + pepper

Scrub the beets, and then steam them in their skins for about 30 minutes. Cool the beets, then remove their skins.

Mix the honey, vinegar, and cornstarch in a saucepan and boil. Add the cooked beets, cloves and a bit of salt and pepper. Simmer over low heat for 5 minutes. Serve.

MAKES 4 SERVINGS

LEVEL 2: LESS SIMPLE

Cyclops Salad

If you bring this surprising salad to a potluck, you will receive surprising compliments. Even people who do not normally eat vegetables enjoy this sweet, crunchy delight. Go on, try it!

3 hard-boiled eggs, peeled
8 oz. crushed pineapple, drained
½ cup plain yogurt
2 tablespoon lemon juice
1 tablespoon honey or sugar
Cinnamon
Nutmeg
4 cups carrots, grated (Knuckle Alert!)
½ cup raisins
¼ cup walnuts, chopped

For Dressing: Combine pineapple, yogurt, lemon juice, honey, cinnamon and nutmeg. Taste.

Add carrots, raisins, and walnuts to above dressing and toss. Arrange the carrot salad on 6 plates. With a spoon, make a hole in the center of each salad. Cut each hard-boiled egg in half the short way. Now place each egg "eye" in the center.

P.S. One thing is sure. You can make this carrot salad with or without its egg eyeball.

MAKES 6 SERVING

LEVEL 3: CHALLENGING

Leafy Green Salad with Vegetation

Let us alone. This is not lettuce alone.

This salad can be made with different sorts of vegetables, not just the ones listed. For example, try tomatillos, radishes, snap peas or steamed asparagus. Add some tuna, turkey or chicken if you like. Many people enjoy Ranch dressing, but some people don't.

6 cherry or yellow pear-shaped tomatoes
1 large carrot
1 medium-size cucumber
1 head romaine lettuce
1 red or green bell pepper
4 hard-boiled eggs (orbs)
Optional: Cubed cooked ham, chicken breast, and cheddar cheese,
Ranch dressing

Remove the earthy end of the lettuce head and throw it away. Better yet, add it to your compost pile. Wash lettuce leaves in cold water. Dry the leaves in a salad spinner (or pat dry with a clean kitchen towel). Tear or cut the leaves into bite-sized pieces. Toss them into a large salad bowl.

Peel and grate the carrot (activate "Knuckle Alert"). Peel and slice the cucumber. Cut the bell pepper into squares. Unite these vegetables with the tomatoes and with the lettuce. Now add ham, chicken, and/or cheese if you please. Slice the hard-boiled egg orbs. Add these slices to the salad. Serve with dressing.

SERVES 4

LEVEL 2: LESS SIMPLE

39

Red-Flecked Potato Salad

Potato salad often has too much mayonnaise. Add a small bit first, mix, then taste. Apply additional lubrication (mayo) if desired.

4 cups diced & cooked small red potatoes (1 quart)
3 tablespoons sweet pickle relish
1 cup diced celery
1½ teaspoons salt
¼ teaspoon pepper
1/8 teaspoon mustard
2 hard-boiled eggs (orbs), sliced
½ to 2/3 cup mayonnaise

To cook potatoes: Scrub them. Place them in a pot with cold, salted water. Boil, then lower the heat and cook until tender, about 15-30 minutes.

Toss together the cooked potatoes, relish, and celery. Sprinkle with salt and pepper. Mix. Add eggs, mustard, and mayonnaise. Repeat mixing.

Have somebody taste the salad, preferably a human. Depending upon the results, initiate the process of salt and pepper seasoning.

SERVES 6

LEVEL 2: LESS SIMPLE

Space Cadet Carrots

Even airheads will remember to eat these sweet carrots. They're that good.

3 carrots, peeled and chopped
3 tablespoons butter
1 tablespoon maple syrup, brown sugar, or honey

Cut carrots into circular slices.

Boil a pot of water. Lower the carrot circles into the boiling water. A slotted spoon helps with this task.

Boil 5 minutes. Drain carrots in colander.

Put carrots into serving bowl. Top with butter. Add 1 tablespoon of syrup, brown sugar, or honey (not a tablespoon of each). Serve.

SERVES 4

LEVEL 2: LESS SIMPLE

41

Optimal Health Hummus Dip

Good for you? Check. Good tasting? Check.

If your hummus seems too dry, add more olive oil or a bit of water. You can eat this tasty dip by itself, in a pita pocket, or with vegetables and tortilla chips. For a burst of color, garnish the dip with chopped parsley or a sprinkle of paprika. "Chickpea" is another name for the garbanzo bean.

1 15 oz. can garbanzo beans
1 garlic clove, minced
¼ cup olive oil
1 tablespoon + 1 teaspoon lemon juice
1 teaspoon cumin
½ teaspoon salt
1 teaspoon tahini (sesame seed paste)

Suggested Sides:
Pita bread
Vegetables slices--cucumber, carrots, celery
Cauliflower and broccoli

Put all the hummus ingredients into a food processor. Blend until smooth. Taste. Adjust seasonings if you wish.

Spread on a sandwich or serve with Suggested Sides.

MAKES ABOUT 2 CUPS

LEVEL 1: EASY

Foodasaurus

DropBob

PartyPop

FinHin

Wingaling

43

Gravitational Guacamole

You can organize an entire meal around this glorious green dip. Guacamole goes great with tortilla chips, baked potatoes, eggs, or inside a cheese sandwich.

2 ripe avocados
1 tablespoon cilantro leaves, finely chopped
1 clove garlic, minced
1 tablespoon of fresh lime or lemon juice
½ teaspoon ground cumin
¼ teaspoon cayenne
½ teaspoon salt
Pepper

Carefully cut the avocados in half and remove the pits. Scoop out the insides and put them into a glass or stainless steel bowl. Mash the avocado with a fork or a potato masher. Add lime or lemon juice, cumin, cayenne, salt, and pepper. Mix. Then add the cilantro and garlic.

When ready to store, place plastic wrap directly on the surface of the guacamole to keep it from turning ugly. Then refrigerate until ready to eat.

SERVES 2-4

*"Gravitation" is the occurrence that gives objects weight. For instance, gravitation keeps the Earth and the other planets in their orbits around the Sun. Gravity is also the thing that keeps us on the ground instead of floating up into space.

LEVEL 1: EASY

Supernova Salsa

This simple salsa is so good that it might overshadow its fellow side dishes. If you like your salsa very hot, add more peppers. Remember to wash your hands before and *after* chopping them, (and before touching any sensitive parts of your body).

28-ounce can of whole peeled tomatoes, drained
¼ cup onion, chopped
3 garlic cloves, chopped
¼ cup fresh cilantro, chopped
2 teaspoons salt
2 teaspoons pepper
2 teaspoons chili powder
2 teaspoons cumin
Optional: 1 chopped jalapeno or 2 chopped Serrano chile peppers, seeds and membranes removed
Optional: squeeze of lemon

Put all the ingredients into a blender. Blend the salsa until it looks good to you. If you want spicier salsa, add the chopped Serrano or jalapeno peppers now. Taste, and squeeze in some lemon juice if desired.

Using Fresh Tomatoes:
Feel free to substitute 4 fresh, ripe, chopped tomatoes for the canned ones. It is a good idea to cut tomatoes in half, then to squeeze out the seeds before chopping.

SERVES 2-4

* A supernova produces a burst of energy that may actually outshine its entire host galaxy before fading from view.

LEVEL 2: LESS SIMPLE

Cosmic Soup

Contrary to its name, this Italian-inspired cosmic soup takes approximately one hour to make, not billions of years. This soup tastes a lot like the Italian soup "minestrone."

1 medium onion, chopped
1 stalk celery, diced
1 carrot, sliced
3 tablespoons margarine, oil, or butter
1 potato
1 16 oz. can diced tomatoes
2 16 oz. cans broth (any kind)
1 teaspoon dry basil or 2 teaspoons fresh basil, chopped
½ cup uncooked macaroni or other pasta
2 small zucchini, sliced
1 16 oz. can kidney beans, drained
Salt + pepper

In large saucepan over medium heat, cook onion, celery, and carrot in margarine, oil, or butter. Stir until onion is soft but not brown. Add potato, tomatoes, broth and basil. Boil. Reduce heat to simmer. Cover and simmer for 15 minutes.

Add macaroni and zucchini. Cook 10 minutes more. Add kidney beans and simmer 5 minutes, until tender. Add salt and pepper. Add Parmesan cheese on top.

SERVES 6

*Cosmic soup is a blurry concept. It's all the stuff that makes up the universe, I think. Maybe you could ask your parents?

LEVEL 2: LESS SIMPLE

Sublime Lime Soup

This is one awe-inspiring chicken, rice, and tortilla soup! The recipe hails from Mexico's Yucatan Peninsula.

Corn tortilla chips
2 boneless chicken breasts, chopped (certified organic chicken is best)
1 onion, chopped
2 cloves garlic, chopped
½ teaspoon black pepper
½ teaspoon cinnamon
½ teaspoon allspice
1 teaspoon oregano
1 cup rice, any kind
4 cups chicken broth
2 cups water
1 tomato, chopped
2 tablespoons lime juice (fresh is best)
1 4 oz. can green chilies

Place chopped chicken, onion, garlic, spices, oregano, rice, and broth into a pot. Add 2 cups water to the soup. Boil. Remove any foam that may arise. Reduce heat. Cover. Simmer 30 minutes.

Add chopped tomato, lime juice, and chilies. Repeat simmering for 10 minutes, until rice is soft. Place 3 tortilla chips into individual soup bowls. Add soup. Serve with slices of lime and additional tortilla chips.

SERVES 4

LEVEL 2: LESS SIMPLE

Lift-Off Lentil Soup

This soup is wholesome, hearty, and exceptional. Lentils are quick to cook. If that were not enough, each lentil resembles a tiny spaceship.

2 cups lentils
2 quarts water
2 teaspoons salt
2 carrots, diced
1 onion, diced
2 stalks celery, diced
2 tablespoons butter
Salt +pepper

Spread 2 cups of dry lentils onto a cookie sheet in order to inspect them. Make sure that no dirt or rocks sneak into your soup. When you have confirmed that the lentils are debris-free, put them into a bowl. Cover with cold water. Soak overnight.

After approximately 8 hours, drain the lentils. Put the lentils and the accompanying vegetables into a soup pot with salted water. Bring to a boil. Reduce heat. Simmer until lentils are tender (approximately 1½ hours). Add butter and seasonings to flavor further. Serve.

SERVES 8

LEVEL 1: EASY

Red Giant Soup

Some Earthlings call this cold, red soup *gazpacho*. They also call it "delicious." If you prefer a spicier soup, add more Tabasco sauce.

6 ripe tomatoes, chopped or 1 28 oz. can of diced tomatoes
1 red onion, finely chopped (optional)
1 cucumber, peeled & chopped (English cucumbers are nice)
1 sweet red bell pepper chopped (don't include seeds)
1 clove garlic, minced
¼ cup red wine vinegar
¼ cup olive oil
2 tablespoons freshly squeezed lemon juice
2 teaspoons sugar
Salt and fresh ground pepper to taste
2 or more drops of Tabasco sauce to taste
4 cups tomato juice

Combine all ingredients in a blender. Puree to desired consistency. Taste. Place in a plastic or ceramic storage container but not a metal one. (Metal reacts badly with the acidic tomatoes.) Cover tightly. Chill 1 hour. Serve.

SERVES 8

LEVEL 2: LESS SIMPLE

Making Dirt *(food for your garden)*

Don't throw away your leftover food scraps. Turn them into dirt instead.

Make a compost pile, perhaps in the back corner of your yard.

Add brown things to the heap, like hay, dried leaves and straw.

Now add fresh stuff like green lawn clippings and the parts of vegetables that you won't eat.

Wet the pile with water. Lift the pile with a shovel and turn it over.

Wait for a few weeks. Add a bit of water each week, and then mix the pile again.

Wait some more.

Watch for steam rising as the compost mound heats up.

The dirt is done. Add this new soil to your garden.

Compost is good for plants, good for you, and good for the Earth.

LEVEL 1: EASY

Positively Charged Pesto

This garlicky green sauce always makes people feel good. Serve it as a dip for bread, or over pasta for a tasty, green "Martian-style Macaroni". Pesto also makes a far-out pizza sauce.

3 cloves garlic
2 cups fresh basil leaves
2½ tablespoons pine nuts
Dash of salt and pepper
½ cup olive oil
½ cup Parmesan cheese, grated

Peel and chop garlic. Wash, dry, and remove stems from basil leaves. Grate Parmesan cheese if need be (if the cheese is not already grated).

Put the garlic into the blender or food processor. Mince at low speed. Stop the machine and add the basil leaves, pine nuts, and a shake of salt and pepper. Blend again, and then stop. Drizzle in the olive oil. Blend again. Stop again.

Now add the Parmesan cheese. Blend again. Pesto is now complete. Cover and refrigerate or freeze the pesto until ready to use.

MAKES 2 CUPS

LEVEL 1: EASY

Realistic Corn Fritters

According to recent inspections, the following fritters appear to be valid. Don't skimp on the peanut oil. It's what gives these little cakes their super special something. You could add chopped red bell pepper to the batter, if you wish.

2 eggs
1 cup milk
1 tablespoon honey
1 12 oz. can corn
2 tablespoons peanut oil
1½ cups flour
1 tablespoon baking powder
½ teaspoon salt
Pepper
More peanut oil for frying

Beat an egg into a large bowl. Stir in the milk, honey, corn, and 2 tablespoons of peanut oil. Whisk in flour, baking powder, salt, and a shake of pepper.

Heat 2 tablespoons of peanut oil in a frying pan. When oil is hot, drop batter by spoonfuls into hot pan. Exercise extreme caution! Oil may splatter. Fry fritters until golden brown (2 minutes per side). Drain fritters on paper towels. Serve.

MAKES 24 FRITTERS

LEVEL 1: EASY

Automatic Acorn Squash

When paired with honey or maple syrup, squash becomes a sweet and delicious treat.

3 Acorn Squash, halved to make six squash "bowls"
6 teaspoons of butter
6 teaspoons of honey or maple syrup
6 tablespoons of brown sugar
Salt & pepper

Preheat oven to 375°F.

Cut each acorn squash in half. Scoop out the seeds with a spoon.

Into each half-squash add 1 teaspoon butter, 1 teaspoon honey or maple syrup, 1 tablespoon brown sugar, and a shake of salt and pepper.

Place these squash-bowls with the cut side up onto a greased cookie sheet. Bake for 1 hour or until tender. To check completion level, please poke the hot squash with a fork, not your finger.

SERVES 4-6

LEVEL 1: EASY

Sputnik Spuds

This heavenly meal will orbit the dinner table quickly.

6 russet baking potatoes
Salt and pepper
2½ cups pasta sauce
Suggested toppings: sour cream, butter, chopped olives, chopped green
peppers, cooked bacon, chopped
½ cup shredded Parmesan cheese
2 cups shredded cheddar, jack, or mozzarella cheese

Preheat the oven to 400°F.

Scrub the potatoes. Poke holes into each one to let the steam escape Bake for 55 minutes. Remove potatoes from the oven and let them cool. Cut them in half the long way. Scoop out the interior portion, leaving a thin potato wall. (Save the inside of the potatoes for another meal. They make excellent mashed potatoes.)

Arrange the hollowed-out skins on a greased baking sheet. Apply a light shake of salt and pepper to the insides of the skins.

Spoon the pizza sauce into each of the hollowed-out potato skins. Sprinkle one or more of the *Suggested Toppings* over the sauce. Add the Parmesan cheese and the other cheese, too. Bake for 15 minutes. Cool for 10 minutes before serving.

SERVES 6

* *In 1957, the Soviet Union sent Sputnik I into space. It was the world's first artificial satellite. Sputnik took about 98 minutes to go around the Earth.*

LEVEL 2: LESS SIMPLE

Sunshine Sides

For maximum freshness, eat vegetables raw and straight from the garden. When you want your vegetables warm and seasoned, go full speed ahead with the recipes below.

Sunshine Broccoli

1½ pounds broccoli, chopped
1 tablespoon vegetable oil
3 tablespoons soy sauce
3 tablespoons hot water
2 teaspoons brown sugar

Mix the soy sauce, hot water, and brown sugar in bowl. Heat the oil in a wok or frying pan. Add broccoli and cook 5 minutes, stirring continually.

Add the sauce ingredients to the broccoli. Cover with pot lid and cook for 5 minutes more. Serve with Wind-Up Sesame Noodles or with rice.

Sunshine Zucchini

3 small zucchini or 1 large
1 tablespoon oil or butter
Garlic powder
Salt
Soy sauce

Slice the zucchini any which way you like. I like the look of circles and half-circles. Heat oil or butter in a frying pan. When hot, add the zucchini. Stir for 5 minutes. Add a shake of garlic powder, then a bit of soy sauce or salt. Serve.

Sunshine Corn

4 Ears of Corn
Butter
Salt and Pepper

Pull off the leafy husks from the corn. Make sure to get off as much of the silky strings as possible. Boil a big pot of water. Carefully drop the corn into the hot water. Cook for 3 minutes.

Remove the ears of corn from the water (use long tongs, or to ask a grown-up for help). Rub butter on the corn and shake on some salt.

LEVEL 1: EASY

Nuts and Bolts

MAIN DISHES

Mechanic's Favorite Grilled Cheese

A grilled cheese sandwich with a bowl of soup provides a warm, enjoyable meal especially on a rainy day. For an added fun factor, take out the cookie cutters and make star-shaped or circle-shaped sandwiches.

And please remember: whenever a problem seems too difficult or complicated to fix, slow down. Breathe deeply, and let the recipe guide you.

2 slices bread
1 slice cheese any kind you like
Margarine or butter, softened, or mayonnaise

Put cheese between two slices of bread. Ask an adult for help if the need arises.

Spread the outside of bread with softened butter, margarine, or mayonnaise. Put the sandwich into an electric sandwich maker. Follow machine instructions until cooking is complete.

OR,

Lightly brown the sandwich in a skillet over a low flame. When the cheese has melted, transfer the sandwich to a plate.

MAKES 1 SANDWICH

LEVEL 1: EASY

Flying Saucer Mini Pizza

Pizza is a versatile vehicle. No wonder pizza is one of Planet Earth's favorite delicacies. Make this easy pizza after school or at a sleepover. Add any toppings you like: sliced olives, crumbled feta cheese, or bell peppers, for example. Use cheddar, asiago, jack, or gruyere cheese in place of mozzarella.

1 bagel, English muffin or 2 slices of bread
Pizza sauce or spaghetti sauce (don't forget the possibility of pesto)
Shredded Mozzarella cheese

Add sauce to the surface of each bagel, English muffin or bread slice. Apply the cheese. Heat in a microwave oven for 30 seconds, or toast the assembly in a toaster oven. Watch so that the cheese does not burn.

MAKES 2

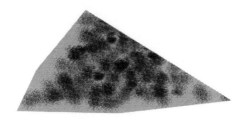

LEVEL 1: EASY

Super Subs

A submarine sandwich looks like a submarine, but it tastes different. Most humans like the flavor of bread, cheese, and meat more than metal. Robots prefer metal.

4 hot dog buns or French rolls
¼ cup mayonnaise
12 slices salami
12 slices ham
4 slices cheddar cheese
4 slices provolone cheese
4-8 slices dill pickles (you can buy sliced pickles)
Lettuce leaves

Open hot dog buns or French rolls. Apply a layer of mayonnaise. Insert provolone, salami, cheddar cheese, ham, and pickles. Add the lettuce leaf.

Press down to compact each sandwich. Otherwise, a mess will result.

MAKES 4

LEVEL 1: EASY

Pigs in Spaceships

I cannot verify that pigs travel in space, but I have heard some rumors. Experiment with homemade pizza dough, or try biscuit, and/or bread dough.

6 hot dogs, frankfurters, veggie dogs, or sausage links
1 can (10 oz.) refrigerated crescent roll dough

Preheat the oven to 400°F. Grease one cookie sheet.

Separate the dough into individual pieces. Wrap the dough around the hot dog. Enclose it as much as possible.

Place on greased cookie sheet. Bake for 11 minutes (or according to dough package instructions).

                                        MAKES 6 SPACE PIGS

LEVEL 1: EASY

Dr. Spockoli's Broccoli Casserole

Interstellar physician Dr. Spockoli recommends that humans eat green vegetables (and other-colored vegetables, too). This cheesy dish could easily be made with cooked butternut squash pieces in place of the broccoli.

1 8-oz. package wide egg noodles, cooked and drained
2 10-oz. packages frozen chopped broccoli, cooked--or use fresh
broccoli (It's even better. Save ¼ cup cooking water for later use)
½ cup cheddar cheese
2 tablespoons butter
1 tablespoon flour
¾ cup milk
½ teaspoon salt
1 teaspoon Worcestershire sauce (pronounced Woos-ti-sher)

Preheat the oven to 350°F.

Combine the cooked noodles and cooked. Mix in the grated cheddar cheese.

Melt the butter in a saucepan. Add flour and stir until thickened. Add milk. Stir constantly. Add salt, Worcestershire sauce, and reserved broccoli water. (Did you accidentally toss the cooking water? Just use regular water.)

Simmer and stir until thick. Pour the sauce over the noodle-broccoli mixture. Blend thoroughly. Bake in a greased 9x13-inch casserole dish for 30 minutes.

SERVES 6

LEVEL 2: LESS SIMPLE

Androids Dream of Almond Chicken (& Sometimes Tofu)

It's true. I have read the reports. Serve this dish with a mound of rice. Sliced oranges make a nice side dish.

Steamed rice
1½ pounds boneless chicken breasts (certified organic chicken is best)
OR 1½ pounds firm tofu
1/3 cup peanut oil
2 cups celery, chopped
1 cup canned water chestnuts, sliced
¼ cup water
¼ lb. snow peas, stems removed
Soy sauce
1 teaspoon cornstarch
2 tablespoons water
1 cup roasted almonds

Follow rice package directions to make 6 servings of rice. Set the rice aside.

Cut the chicken or tofu into small cubes. Heat oil in large skillet or wok. Brown chicken or tofu rapidly. Add celery, water chestnuts, and water. Cover and cook for 7 minutes.

Add the snow peas to the other vegetables. Cover the pan again. Cook for 5 minutes. Mix the cornstarch and water in separate bowl. Add to the vegetables. Stir until sauce becomes thick. Sprinkle with almonds before serving.

MAKES 6 SERVINGS

LEVEL 2: LESS SIMPLE

63

Uni-Pot Spaghetti

Do you own only one pot? If so, this dish is for you. You can easily add ground beef, turkey, or vegetarian crumbles. If you decide to include one of these items, begin by heating oil in a pot. Then add the meat or meat substitute, brown it, and proceed with the recipe as written.

2½ cups water
1 16 oz. can of tomato sauce
1 teaspoon dried oregano
½ teaspoon dried basil
¼ teaspoon salt
¼ teaspoon garlic powder
¼ teaspoon pepper
6 ounces spaghetti (somewhat less than half of a 1 lb. box)*
Parmesan cheese

Put water, tomato sauce, oregano, basil, salt, garlic powder, and pepper into a large frying pan with lid (with meat or meat substitute). Turn heat to high. Cook uncovered, until the sauce bubbles.

Break the spaghetti in half and add it to the pan. Turn the heat to low. Cover and simmer for 30 minutes. Stir the spaghetti every 10 minutes or so. Exercise caution when removing lid! Watch for burning-hot steam and for hot water that may drip from the lid onto your arm or bare foot (Shoes are recommended while cooking).

Serve with Parmesan cheese.

* There are 16oz. in one pound.

SERVES 2-4

LEVEL 1: EASY

Bubbling Blue Nachos

You could make this dish with yellow or white tortilla chips. Blue corn, however, contains a higher protein value. Some people also claim that indigo (blue) corn can heal. Please report back.

2 cups refried beans (one 16 oz. can)
1 cup salsa
8 cups blue tortilla corn chips
2 cups shredded cheese (jack or cheddar work well)
Suggested Toppings include: sliced black olives, guacamole, chopped
green peppers, sour cream, chopped onion, chopped tomato, sliced
jalapeno peppers

Mix the beans and salsa together in a bowl. Arrange the chips on a large microwavable platter. Top the chips with the bean mixture. Sprinkle on the shredded cheese.

Microwave on high for 2 minutes or until the cheese melts. You could also make this dish in a toaster oven, using the proper pan.

Add one or more of the *Suggested Toppings*.   SERVES 4

LEVEL 1: EASY

Curried Tofu Substance

This substance tastes a lot like egg salad, only without the eggs. Serve it as a salad on top of lettuce leaves, or spread it on bread for a sandwich.

4 tablespoons mayonnaise (use soy mayo if you want to keep the dish vegan)
2 tablespoons mango chutney
2 teaspoons curry powder
¼ teaspoon salt
Pepper
1 (14-oz.) package firm tofu
2 stalks celery, diced
Optional: red grapes, scallions, walnuts, grated carrot, raisins, and sunflower seeds

Mix together the mayonnaise, chutney, curry powder, salt and pepper in a large bowl. Crumble the tofu and add it to the bowl. Stir in the celery, and any of the optional ingredients that appeal to you. Cover and chill for at least one hour so the flavors can develop. Used as a sandwich spread, it's very good on toasted bread.

MAKES 5 SERVINGS

LEVEL 1: EASY

Earth's Finest Tofu Triangles

Special Report: Best-ever tofu morsels have arrived on Planet Earth.

1 Block of Firm Tofu
¼ cup tamari or soy sauce
Two handfuls of Nutritional Yeast
Optional: ginger or garlic powder

Cut the big block of tofu into three smaller pieces, then cut each piece into 4 to 8 triangles. Put the tofu into a container with a lid. Pour some tamari over the tofu, put on the lid onto the container, and give it a shake.

Let the tamari soak in for at least 20 minutes. This can be refrigerated all day if you want. But do give the container another shake at some point.

Preheat the oven to 375°F. Oil a baking sheet.

Drain any remaining tamari off of the tofu, if there is any. Toss the tofu with a handful of nutritional yeast. Then cover the container and shake it. Then open the lid, add another handful of yeast, and shake again.

Place the triangles onto the greased baking sheet. Lightly spray some oil onto the top of the tofu.

Bake for 10-15 minutes. Turn the triangles over with a spatula, then bake them for another 10 minutes.

Variation: You can add ginger or garlic powder to the tamari marinade. A sprinkle of kosher salt before baking also imparts the tofu with a special flavor.

LEVEL 1: EASY

Tectonic Plates of Teriyaki Beef

If Terrence always wants to change seats with Cecile, then you should make this meal because it shifts around naturally. That is a joke. (You will need a slow cooker for this recipe. That is not a joke.) Serve atop rice. Basmati rice is nice.

2½ pounds flank steak, or "stir-fry beef"
1 20 oz. can pineapple chunks, drained - reserve 1/2 cup of the juice
¼ cup soy sauce
½ teaspoon dry ginger powder
2 teaspoons garlic, minced
2 tablespoons sugar
3 tablespoons cornstarch
3 tablespoons water

Combine the beef, soy sauce, ginger, sugar, garlic, and pineapple juice in a slow-cooking device. Cook on low heat for 7 hours.

Mix the cornstarch with water. Turn the slow cooker's setting to high. Add the cornstarch mixture and the pineapple chunks. Cook for 10 minutes. Serve over rice.

SERVES 4

* Tectonic plates are massive slabs of solid rock on the outer surface of the Earth. During earthquakes, the plates move. Most of the world's active volcanoes occur in places where two plates meet one another.

LEVEL 2: LESS SIMPLE

Meteor Meatballs

Some meatball ideas: 1. Insert a toothpick into each meatball. Serve on a platter as an appetizer. 2. Add spaghetti sauce to meatballs and serve over pasta. 3. Place 3 meatballs into a hot dog bun and make a sandwich. 4. Serve meatballs on rice.

1½ pounds ground beef
1/3 cup uncooked rice
½ cup canned tomatoes
1 large onion, finely chopped
3 tablespoons fresh parsley, minced
Salt and pepper
2 eggs, beaten
6 cups bouillon or broth (Bouillon cubes=broth cubes. Dissolve 6 cubes into 6 cups hot water.)

Combine all ingredients except bouillon. Knead with clean hands. Roll lightly into 1½-inch balls (about ping-pong ball size).

Bring bouillon-infused water to a boil. Drop in the meatballs. Reduce the heat to simmer. Cover the pot. Cook for 25 minutes. Cooked meatballs will rise to the surface.

SERVES 4

LEVEL 2: LESS SIMPLE

69

Wind-Up Sesame Noodles

Serve this dish with steamed broccoli to obtain maximum benefits. Wind the noodles around your fork prior to eating to achieve ultimate happiness.

1 package linguine or spaghetti noodles
½ cup sesame oil
7 tablespoons soy sauce
3 tablespoons balsamic vinegar
3½ tablespoons brown sugar
2 teaspoons salt
2 teaspoons chili oil
½ teaspoon ginger
1 garlic clove, chopped small
Salt

Mix the sauce ingredients together. Stir to dissolve the sugar. Set aside.

Bring a large pot of water to a boil. Add the salt. Cook the noodles according to the package directions. When the buzzer sounds, pour the noodles into a colander to drain (remember your pot holders!).

Rinse the noodles under cold water to stop them from cooking more and to remove excess starch. Shake the colander to and fro. Then toss the noodles with the sauce and serve.

SERVES 4

LEVEL 2: LESS SIMPLE

A Fettuccini Named Alfredo

I met him once. He sang marvelously.

This recipe is as a favorite of children and adults. However, keep in mind that the young people may not like as much nutmeg and pepper as their older counterparts.

3 tablespoons light cream or whipping cream, at room temperature
14 oz. package fettuccini noodles
1/3 cup grated Parmesan cheese
1 tablespoon butter
Pepper
Ground nutmeg

Cook the fettuccini noodles according to the package directions. Drain noodles well. Return the fettuccini to the empty cooking pot. Add the cream, Parmesan cheese, and the butter.

Mix well. Transfer noodles to a serving dish. Sprinkle with pepper and nutmeg. Do not allow fettuccini to sit for a long time. Serve it immediately (or as soon as possible).

MAKES 4 SERVINGS

LEVEL 1: EASY

Powder-Free Macaroni

Not instant is not impossible. This macaroni-dish is designed to please, with actual genuine, shredded cheese.

1 cup elbow or shell macaroni
1 cup milk
3 tablespoons flour
Salt and pepper to taste
2 tablespoons butter
1 cup shredded cheddar cheese

Boil a large pot of salted water. Add the elbows or shells (macaroni). Cook for about 9 minutes. Drain the noodles. Set aside.

Combine the milk, flour, salt and pepper in a microwave-safe bowl. Mix the ingredients until no lumps remain. Add the butter and cheese. Microwave on high for 5 minutes. Heat Alert! Remove the bowl *very* carefully and stir again until the cheese mixture looks smooth.

Microwave the mixture for an additional 4 minutes. Remember the bowl will be hot! Stir cheese sauce again. No lumps should remain.

Add the cooked pasta to the cheese sauce. Stir. Serve.

SERVES 4-5

LEVEL 1: EASY

Quasar Quiche

Quasars (quasi-stellar radio sources) emit large amounts of energy in space whereas quiches send forth power at home. You may want to increase your own energy output (and input) by including nutrient-rich vegetables in your quiche.

10" unbaked pie shell (frozen or made fresh)
1 tablespoon butter, softened or 1 teaspoon mustard
1 cup grated cheese, any kind
1 tablespoon flour
¼ teaspoon salt
Pepper
Pinch of nutmeg
6 eggs
2 cups milk (or cream for a richer tasting quiche)
Optional: vegetables, like chopped spinach, mushrooms or onions

Preheat the oven to 450°F.

Apply a thin layer of butter or mustard onto the bottom of the pie shell. Sprinkle on cheese. Add some of the *Optional vegetables* if desired.

Mix the dry ingredients, and then add the eggs and the milk. Beat until mixed. Pour the egg mixture on top of cheese. Bake for 10 minutes. Lower the heat to 325°F. Bake for 25 more minutes.

Remove the quiche when a knife inserted emerges clean. Let the quiche sit for 10 minutes so that it can firm up before serving.

SERVES 4-6

LEVEL 1: EASY

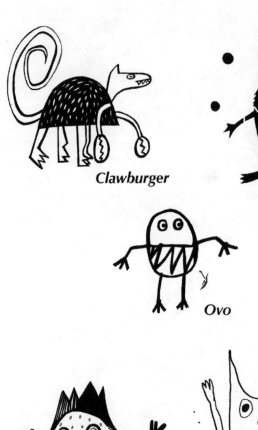

Clawburger

AppleJuggler

Ovo

RoyalBurger

CheeseHead

74

Zany Zucchini Squares

One zucchini plant yields many offspring. Use three of the vegetables here. You can buy prepared bread crumbs at the grocery store, or you can toast the end slices from your favorite bread and crush them to make your own.

3 small zucchini, sliced
1 onion, chopped (optional)
4 eggs
½ cup milk
2 cups cheese, shredded (Monterey Jack works well)
½ teaspoon salt
2 teaspoons baking powder
3 tablespoons flour
½ cup bread crumbs
Butter

Preheat the oven to 350°F.

Put the zucchini slices into a pot with a small amount of water. Cover the pot. Cook over medium heat for approximately 5 minutes. Carefully drain and cool the zucchini.

Beat the eggs in a big bowl. Add the milk, grated cheese, salt, baking powder, flour, and onion if using. Stir in the zucchini.

Pour everything into buttered 9 x 13-inch casserole dish. Scatter breadcrumbs evenly onto the surface. Dot the surface with butter. Bake for 38-40 minutes.

SERVES 6-8

LEVEL 2: LESS SIMPLE

Polar Chili

Polar Chili satisfies most of the people some of the time. You can make this dish meatless or meat-full. To create an impressive Tamale Pie, put the chili into a pie pan and top it with Mission Control Cornbread batter. Bake the pie in the oven for 30 minutes at 400°F.

1½ pounds ground beef, "veggie crumbles," or ground turkey
1 medium onion, chopped
1 medium bell pepper, chopped
1 teaspoon olive oil
3 16 oz. cans kidney beans
1½ cups frozen or fresh corn (or 1 can)
1 16 oz. can diced tomatoes
1 small can tomato sauce
1 tablespoon chili powder
2 teaspoons cumin

Heat the meat in a large pot. When using a meat substitute, add I tablespoon of oil to the pan first. Stir and cook until browned.

Mix all the other ingredients into the pot and heat to boiling. Reduce the heat to low and cook for 1 hour.

SERVES 4-6

LEVEL 2: LESS SIMPLE

Frenetic Fried Rice

To increase the already-high excitement level of this dish, add more vegetables, cooked meat like chicken or ham, or tofu.

2 tablespoons oil
2 beaten eggs
½ teaspoon ginger or 1 teaspoon fresh grated ginger
3 cups cold, cooked rice
2 cups chopped Chinese cabbage (also called Napa cabbage)
2 tablespoons soy sauce
1 tablespoon water
Optional ingredients: ½ cup cooked tofu, or chicken. You could also add lightly cooked vegetables like carrots, peas, mushrooms, green onions, etc.

In a large skillet, heat one tablespoon oil over medium heat. Add the eggs and cook without stirring until the eggs appear somewhat firm. Remove the cooked eggs and put them on a plate. Cut the cooked egg into small pieces.

Heat the remaining oil over medium heat. Add the tofu, meat and/or vegetables. Add the ginger. Cook for about 3 minutes.

Stir in the cooked rice, the cabbage, and the egg strips. Sprinkle with soy sauce and 1 tablespoon of water. Cook 4 more minutes. Toss the rice mixture gently.

SERVES 4

LEVEL 3: CHALLENGING

desserts desserts desserts desserts desserts

79

Crater Cookies

Use your thumb to punch new craters onto the surface of each cookie. If you wish to fill the craters with chocolate kisses instead of jam, go right ahead.

1¾ cups butter
1½ cups brown sugar
3 egg yolks (retain the whites)
1½ teaspoon vanilla
4 cups flour
1 teaspoon salt

Preheat the oven to 350°F.

In a large bowl, cream the butter and brown sugar. Mix until fluffy (an electric mixer comes in handy here). Beat in the egg yolks and the vanilla. In another bowl, combine the flour and salt. Add to the other mixture.

Slightly eat the egg whites in a small bowl. Roll the dough into 1-inch balls. Dip the balls into the egg whites. Place each sphere onto a greased cookie sheet.

Indent the center of each cookie with a clean thumb. Bake for 11 minutes. Cool the cookies for 5 minutes. Fill craters with jam or kisses.

MAKES 3 DOZEN (36 cookies)

* Craters are pits on landforms that are caused by the impact of meteors or other space objects.

LEVEL 2: LESS SIMPLE

Robot Cookies

Robot cookies can be decorated with frosting, candy, sprinkles, and raisins. Start simply and expand exponentially.

2½ cups all-purpose flour
1 teaspoon baking powder
½ teaspoon salt
½ pound (2 sticks) butter, softened
1 cup granulated sugar
2 eggs
2 teaspoons vanilla extract
6 drops green food coloring
Assorted candy decorations

A ROBOT COOKIE

Mix the flour and baking powder in a bowl.

In another bowl, beat the butter, sugar and salt with an electric mixer for 3 minutes. (Or stir ingredients manually.) Add the eggs. Beat again. Add vanilla and food coloring. Mix again. Gradually add the flour mixture. Combine completely.

Divide the dough into 3 parts. Cover each part with plastic wrap. Chill for 2 hours.

Preheat oven to 375°F.

Dust a large, clean cutting board with flour. Roll the dough so that it's about ¼-inch thick. Cut out rectangles or other robotic shapes. Place the cookies onto an ungreased cookie sheet. Decorate with chocolate chips and other candy. Bake for about 8 minutes.

MAKES 24

LEVEL 3: CHALLENGING

Cyclical Chocolate Chip Cookies

You will probably bake these cookies again and again. Add ½ cup raisins or chopped nuts along with the chips if you like.

2 sticks unsalted butter
2¼ cups flour
1 teaspoon salt
1 teaspoon baking soda
¼ cup sugar
1¼ cups brown sugar
2 eggs
2 tablespoons milk
1½ teaspoons vanilla extract
2 cups semisweet chocolate chips

Preheat oven to 375°F.

Melt the butter over low heat or in a microwave-safe bowl in the microwave.

Sift together the flour, salt, and baking soda and set aside.

Pour the melted butter in a large bowl. Add both types of sugar. Using an electric mixer, on medium speed, cream the butter with the sugars. Add the eggs, milk, and the vanilla extract. Mix well.

Gradually add the flour mixture. Mix well. Stir in the chocolate chips.

Make ping-pong sized balls of dough. Put them onto an ungreased cookie sheet about an inch apart. Bake for approximately 11 minutes.

MAKES 6 DOZEN

LEVEL 1: EASY

Peanut Butter Cookie Bytes

These cookie bytes deliver delicious information to your system. This recipe calls for shaping the dough into logs, refrigerating the logs, then slicing them into cookies.

2½ cups flour
1 teaspoon baking powder
1 teaspoon baking soda
1 teaspoon salt
1 cup butter, softened
1 cup creamy peanut butter
1 cup sugar
1 cup brown sugar
2 eggs, beaten
1 teaspoon vanilla

Stir together the flour, baking powder, baking soda, and salt. Set aside.

In large bowl, beat the butter and peanut butter together until smooth. Beat in both sugars. Blend. Beat in eggs and vanilla. Add flour mixture and beat well.

Divide the batter in half and make two logs of dough. Wrap each log in plastic wrap and refrigerate for 2 hours.

Preheat the oven to 350°F.

Slice the logs into semi-thick slices. Place the slices onto an ungreased cookie sheet, 2 inches apart. Bake for 11 minutes.

MAKES 48 BYTES

LEVEL 1: EASY

Cosmonaut Cakes

These nutty cakes are really more like big cookies. In an ideal world, each person would get one.

Serving suggestion: Put the little cakes into a bowl that has been covered with aluminum foil. Then wear your space helmet while distributing.

2 cups butter
1 cup powdered sugar
2 tablespoon vanilla
4½ cups flour
½ teaspoon salt
1½ cups walnuts, finely chopped

Beat the butter, sugar, and vanilla together until fluffy. Combine the flour and salt in separate bowl.

Add flour mixture to the butter mixture. Stir in the nuts. Chill the dough for at least 2 hours.

Preheat the oven to 350°F.

Form the dough into ping-pong sized balls. Bake for 11 minutes. The cakes should not be brown.

Roll the cakes in powdered sugar while still warm (but not too hot).

SERVES 6

LEVEL 2: LESS SIMPLE

Flakey Bakes

Sometimes these chewy coconut delights are referred to as "macaroons."

1 1/3 cups sweetened coconut flakes
1/3 cup sugar
2 tablespoons flour
1/8 teaspoon salt
2 egg whites (Ask an adult to help separate the eggs, or buy "just the whites")
½ teaspoon almond extract

Preheat oven to 325°F.

Combine coconut flakes, sugar, flour and salt in mixing bowl. Stir in egg whites and almond extract. Mix.

Drop by teaspoonfuls onto lightly greased baking sheet. Bake for 23 minutes.

Remove bakes with spatula. Cool on a ceramic plate or a wire rack.

MAKES 18

LEVEL 1: EASY

Powerful Peanut Butter Balls

You can make this dessert during a power outage because you won't need to cook or bake it. As an added bonus, you should regain any lost power within your own system.

2 cups peanut butter
1 cup honey
1 cup wheat germ
1 cup nonfat dry milk powder
1 teaspoon vanilla
2 teaspoons sugar
Optional: coconut flakes, nuts

Mix all of the ingredients together, except for the coconut flakes and the nuts.

Shape into small balls. Roll each ball into the coconut flakes or nuts (or both).

SERVES 8

LEVEL 1: EASY

Chocolate Space Balls

An unknown number of people call these "truffles." Whatever you call them, the balls make a nice gift for people that like chocolate.

1 (8 ounce) package cream cheese, at room temperature
3 cups powdered sugar
3 cups chocolate chips
1 1/2 teaspoons vanilla
Optional: Cocoa powder, extra powdered sugar, chopped nuts

In a large bowl, beat the cream cheese until smooth. Gradually beat in the powdered sugar. Melt the chocolate chips in a microwave oven or over a low flame. Once melted, add the vanilla.

Add this melted chocolate and vanilla mixture to the cream cheese mixture. Combine thoroughly. Refrigerate for 2 hours.

Make small chocolate balls with your clean hands. Roll each ball into cocoa, powdered sugar, or nuts.

Put the space balls onto a cookie sheet lined with wax paper. Freeze them for 2 hours. Cover any leftovers and store them in the refrigerator.

MAKES 60 SPACE BALLS

LEVEL 1: EASY

Bedrock Brownies

These are your basic brownies. If you plan to add nuts *and* chocolate chips, use ½ cup of each.

1/2 cup butter (1 stick)
2 (1 oz.) squares unsweetened chocolate
1 cup sugar
2 eggs, well beaten
1/2 teaspoon vanilla
3/4 cup flour
1/4 teaspoon salt
Optional: 1 cup chopped walnuts, pecans, or chocolate chips

Preheat oven to 350°F.

Melt the butter and chocolate together in a large saucepan (or in the microwave). Remove from heat and stir in the remaining ingredients.

Pour the mixture into a greased and floured 8-inch square pan.

Bake for 28 minutes. Cool. Cut into squares.

SERVES 9

LEVEL 1: EASY

Bionicalorie Brownies

Gain strength! Gain speed! Gain weight! These brownies are ultra-rich.

1 cup butter (2 sticks)
6 (1-oz.) squares unsweetened chocolate
1 ½ cup sugar
3 eggs
½ teaspoon vanilla
1 ½ cups flour
¼ teaspoon salt
Optional: 2 cups mini-marshmallows

Preheat oven to 350°F.

Grease an 8-inch square pan.

Melt the butter and chocolate together in a large saucepan (or in the microwave). Remove from the heat and stir in the remaining ingredients, except for the marshmallows.

Bake for 28-30 minutes. Remove from oven and immediately sprinkle with mini-marshmallows. Cover the pan for a few moments so that the marshmallows begin to melt. Cut when cool.

SERVES 8-12

LEVEL 1: EASY

Light Speed Lemon Bars

These bars will disappear very, very quickly. You could add a shake of powdered sugar on top after baking, but it's not necessary.

1 cup butter
2 cups all-purpose flour
1/2 cup powdered sugar
2 cups white sugar
4 eggs
1 lemon (grate or zest the peel)
6 tablespoon lemon juice
1/2 teaspoon baking powder
1 1/2 cups chopped walnuts
1 tablespoon flour

Preheat the oven to 325°F. Grease a 9 x 13-inch pan.

For the Crust: In a large mixing bowl, beat together the butter, flour, and powdered sugar until fluffy. Smooth the mixture into the pan. Bake for 15 minutes.

For the Filling: In a medium bowl, beat the eggs with sugar. Add the grated lemon rind. Also add 6 tablespoons of lemon juice. Sprinkle 1 tablespoon flour and the baking powder over the mixture. Fold in the nuts. Mix well.

Pour the lemon mixture onto the baked crust. Bake again for 35 minutes. Cool. Cut into bars.

MAKES 12 BARS

* Light speed is approximately 299,792.5 kilometers per second. Wow!

LEVEL 2: LESS SIMPLE

Space Junk Food

Distribute this "junk" around to your friends during the holiday season.

1 box cinnamon graham crackers
½ cup margarine (8 T or 1 stick)
½ cup butter (8 T or 1 stick)
½ cup sugar
Optional: 1 cup chocolate chips

Preheat the oven to 350 degrees.

Overhang a cookie sheet with foil or parchment paper. It should be hanging over the edges. Place one layer of graham crackers on the foil with all of the cracker edges touching.

Melt the margarine and butter together in a pot over a low flame. Do not use the microwave instead.

Once melted, add the sugar and boil the mixture just for 2 minutes. Stir the pot the entire time. Remove the mixture from the heat and pour it over the graham crackers. Spread the mixture over all of the crackers, and bake for 11 minutes.

When you take the Space Junk Food out of the oven, sprinkle the top with chocolate chips. Let the chocolate melt and then spread it over the graham crackers. Cool the dessert. Break the Space Junk Food into small pieces and enjoy.

SERVES 8-10

* Space junk refers to stuff that people have made that still orbit around the Earth, but that have become useless.

LEVEL 2: LESS SIMPLE

Quality-Controlled Carrot Cake

No flaws were discovered during the testing of this recipe. You could serve this cake at a birthday party, or at some other celebration.

1 1/2 cups vegetable oil
1 cup brown sugar
2/3 cup honey
4 eggs
2 1/4 cup flour
1 tablespoon cinnamon
1/2 teaspoon cloves
1/2 teaspoon nutmeg
2 1/2 teaspoons baking soda
1 teaspoon salt
3 cups carrot, grated
10 oz. can crushed pineapple, drained

Preheat the oven to 350°F. Butter and flour a 9 x 13-inch pan.

Combine the oil, sugar, honey, and eggs. Combine the dry ingredients in another bowl. Add them to the oil mixture. Stir in the grated carrots and pineapple. Pour the batter into the greased pan. Bake for 37-40 minutes. Cool. Frost if desired.

Cream Cheese Frosting
12 oz. cream cheese
3 tablespoons melted margarine
1 tablespoon vanilla extract
1 cup powdered sugar

Beat all of the frosting ingredients together until smooth.

SERVES 12

LEVEL 2: LESS SIMPLE

Dark Star Vegan Cupcakes

No milk or eggs are found here. You can top the cupcakes with non-dairy chocolate chips before baking, or frost with the "Creamy" Chocolate Frosting.

1 cup plain soy milk
1 teaspoon apple cider vinegar
1 cup sugar
1/3 cup oil (canola works well)
1 ½ teaspoon vanilla
1 cup flour
1/3 cup good cocoa powder
¾ teaspoon baking soda
½ teaspoon baking powder
¼ teaspoon salt
½ cup vegan chocolate chips

Preheat the oven to 350°F.

Prepare muffin pan with paper liners or by greasing the cups.

In a big bowl, stir together the soy milk and the vinegar. Let it rest for ten minutes. I like to use a kitchen timer.

After ten minutes, add the oil, sugar, and vanilla. Beat well by hand, or with an electric mixer.

In another bowl, stir together the dry ingredients. Slowly add them to the wet mixture. Beat until the batter is nearly smooth. Fold in the chocolate chops. I mean, chocolate chips.

Pour the batter into the muffin cups until you are a half-inch from the top. Bake approximately 20 minutes. A toothpick inserted into the center should emerge clean. Cool the cupcakes. Top with the following non-dairy frosting, if desired.

Creamy Chocolate Frosting

1 cup margarine (Earth Balance is vegan)
4 cups powdered sugar (also called "confectioner's sugar")
1 tablespoon vanilla
4 tablespoons plain soy milk
½ cup cocoa powder
Salt

Beat the margarine until it's creamy. Add a pinch of salt, vanilla, cocoa powder, the sugar, and the soymilk. Beat the frosting for five minutes or until it is fluffy.

MAKES 12

LEVEL 2: LESS SIMPLE

94

Heavy-Duty Popcorn

This popcorn makes a durable and gooey snack. Warning: Upon eating, you may find yourself exclaiming, "Yippee!"

2/3 cup honey
1/2 cup butter
1 cup brown sugar
8 cups plain popped popcorn
1 tablespoon milk

Preheat oven to 375°F.

In a large bowl, mix the honey, butter, brown sugar, and milk. Add popped popcorn. Mix.

Spread onto greased baking sheet. Bake 10 minutes. Alert! Don't let it burn.

SERVES 2-4

LEVEL 1: EASY

95

Adaptable Applesauce

A dessert, a snack, a-mazing!

6 apples
1/2 cup water or apple juice
1/4 teaspoon cinnamon
1/4 cup sugar

Remove the apple cores.

Cut the apples into chunks. Leave on the fiber-filled skins if desired. Put the pieces into a pot. Add water or apple juice, cinnamon, and sugar. Boil.

Lower the heat and simmer covered, until tender. When cool, mash with a fork or blend in the food processor.

SERVES 4

LEVEL 1: EASY

Of Pluto & Peach Crumble

Pluto is not called a planet anymore, yet it remains important. Peach Crumble never was a pie, but it's delicious just the same.

3 cups fresh peaches, sliced
1/4 teaspoon nutmeg
1/2 teaspoon cinnamon
1/3 cup oatmeal
2 tablespoons butter
2 tablespoons oil
2 tablespoons water

Preheat oven to 375°F.

Arrange the peach slices in a pie pan. Sprinkle with cinnamon and nutmeg.

Combine the other ingredients in a bowl. Stir until crumbly.

Sprinkle the crumb mixture over the peaches. Bake for 35 minutes until bubbles appear.

SERVES 6-8

LEVEL 1: EASY

Apricot-Coconut Spheres

Prepare to get sticky while creating these tasty, tangy balls of wonder. You could roll them into logs instead of balls. When done, store them in an airtight container in the freezer or refrigerator.

1 1/2 cups dried apricots
2 cups coconut flakes
2/3 cup sweetened condensed milk
Powdered sugar

Use a food processor. Grind the dried apricots into tiny pieces.

Transfer the apricot bits to another bowl. Add the coconut flakes and the sweetened condensed milk. Blend thoroughly.

Shape the mixture into 1-inch spheres (or logs about 2 inches long). Put some powdered sugar into another bowl. Coat the balls (or logs).

Place the spheres onto baking sheet, but do not bake the balls. Instead, refrigerate them for 2 hours prior to eating.

MAKES 3 DOZEN SPHERES

LEVEL 1: EASY

Push-Button Pumpkin Pie

If you can push a button, you can bake this pie. (It's virtually that easy.)
Top with whipped cream or vanilla ice cream or nothing.

3/4 cup sugar
1 1/2 teaspoons pumpkin pie spice
1/2 teaspoon salt
1 can (15 oz) pumpkin
1 1/4 cups half and half
2 eggs, beaten
1 frozen deep-dish pie crust

Preheat oven to 425°F.

In large bowl, combine the sugar, spice, salt, pumpkin, half-and-half, and the eggs. Pour the mixture into the frozen pie crust.

Bake for 15 minutes. Reduce the oven temperature to 350°F. Bake for an additional 45 minutes, or until a knife inserted near the center emerges clean.

Cool for 2 hours. Refrigerate the pie, or serve it immediately.

MAKES 8 SERVINGS

LEVEL 1: EASY

99

Ideal yet Real Rice Pudding

The power of rice pudding now belongs to you. Serve it well.

1 cup uncooked rice
2 cups water
3 eggs, beaten
2 cups milk
1/2 cup white sugar
1 teaspoon vanilla
1/2 teaspoon salt
1/3 cup raisins
Ground nutmeg

Preheat the oven to 325°F.

Place the uncooked rice in a saucepan. Add 2 cups water.

Boil. Reduce heat to low. Cook uncovered for 25 minutes. Combine the eggs, milk, sugar, vanilla, and salt in a large bowl. Mix well. Carefully stir in the rice and raisins.

Pour the mixture into an 8 x 8-inch square baking dish. Bake uncovered for 30 minutes.

Stir the pudding and sprinkle it with nutmeg.

Put the pan back into the oven and bake for an additional 30 minutes (or until a knife inserted halfway between the edge and the center emerges clean.)

SERVES 2-4

LEVEL 2: LESS SIMPLE

Breadbot Pudding

This bread pudding could be served at breakfast or for dessert with ice cream.

4 eggs, beaten
3/4 cups sugar
½ teaspoon salt
1 teaspoon cinnamon
1/2 teaspoon vanilla
4 cups milk
4 slices buttered bread (use the best quality bread you have)

Preheat oven to 350°F.

Mix together the eggs, sugar, vanilla, and milk. Put the buttered bread slices into an 8-inch square pan and pour the mixture over the bread. Bake the pudding for approximately 45 minutes.

SERVES 4

LEVEL 1: EASY

Intergalactic Ice Cream Pie

This pleasing pie hails from a distant galaxy, but you can locate all of the essential ingredients locally. You could serve the pie with whipped cream.

2 pints ice cream, any flavor
16 chocolate sandwich cookies (like Oreos)
3 tablespoons melted butter
Candy sprinkles, nuts, etc.

Preheat oven to 325°F.

Break the cookies in half. Put them into the bowl of a food processor. Pulse several times until you see small crumbs.

Add the melted butter through the tube while the food processor operates. Run the processor for approximately 15 seconds.

Pat this crumb mixture into the bottom and onto the sides of a pie pan. Bake for 15 minutes. Cool completely.

Scoop the ice cream into a big bowl. Stir the ice cream to soften it. When it is soft but not melted, spoon the ice cream onto the crust. Smooth the surface of the ice cream so that it looks nice. Apply any decorations you like. Freeze for 3 hours. Slice with a warm knife and serve.

SERVES 8

* Galaxies are super-large groups of stars that are found within the universe.

LEVEL 1: EASY

Rocket Pops

Make these for the Fourth of July or at any other time you want a cool, fun treat. Layer the juice in any order that pleases you. Of course, you could create pops with totally different color combinations if you use apple juice or orange juice, for instance.

Red juice (red raspberry, cherry, or cranberry)
Purple Juice (grape or blueberry)
Lemonade or White Grape Juice
Small paper cups or Plastic Popsicle Container/Trays
Wooden Popsicle Sticks

Place several small paper cups onto a baking sheet or use plastic popsicle-making trays instead but you will need to use wooden sticks.

Pour 2 tablespoons of red juice into each cup or popsicle container. Freeze for 2 hours. Remove from freezer and insert a wooden stick into the center of the frozen juice. If it won't stand for some reason, you could cover the top of the cup with plastic wrap and poke the stick through that.

Add 2-3 tablespoons of white juice and freeze again for 2 hours. Remove from freezer and top with a layer purple juice. Lastly, freeze the pops for 3 additional hours. Now the pops are ready to enjoy!

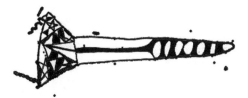

LEVEL 1: EASY

103

Liquid DRINKS

Mercurial Mint Syrup

Like the element mercury, this mint beverage syrup can roll any which way. Add this fresh flavoring to tea, seltzer, or water. (Important: Never consume the element mercury.)

2 cups sugar
2 1/2 cups water
1 cup fresh mint leaves
Juice of 6 lemons
Juice of 2 oranges
Grated rind of 1 orange

Put the sugar and water in a saucepan. Cook over medium heat for 5 minutes. Turn off heat and cool the mixture. Add the fruit juices and the orange rind.

Pour the juice mixture over the fresh, clean, mint leaves. Let the liquid stand for one hour.

Strain the concoction over a bowl to catch the precious syrup. Pour the syrup into a container with a lid. Store in the refrigerator. Throw away or compost the mint leaves and the rind that you caught in the strainer.

How to Use: For each drink serving, fill a glass one-third of the way up with syrup. Then add ice and water, tea, seltzer, or ginger ale.

SERVES 10 - 12

LEVEL 2: LESS SIMPLE

Energizing Horchata

One sip and you will feel compelled to drink more of this sweet rice beverage. Much more. Note: You may want an adult to help you make this recipe.

4 cups milk
8 cups water
4 cinnamon sticks
1/3 cup uncooked rice
3/4 cup sugar
1 tablespoon vanilla

Pulverize the uncooked rice in blender or food processor until it becomes powdery.

Pour the milk into a pot and bring to a boil. Reduce the heat to low and simmer for about 25 minutes, stirring often. Hold a strainer over a large saucepan. Pour the mixture into the strainer so that the liquid goes into the pan. It will be hot so please be careful. Add the water and cinnamon sticks.

Bring to a boil. Then reduce the heat to low and cook for 5 minutes. Turn off the heat and let the pot sit for 15 minutes. Remove the cinnamon sticks carefully with a spoon.

Stir together the rice powder, sugar and vanilla in a bowl. Pour in the milk mixture and blend well. Refrigerate for about 5 hours or overnight. Pour the horchata from the bowl into a pitcher, but don't include the stuff (sediment) that has settled at the bottom of the bowl. Serve the horchata cold over ice.   SERVES 6-8

LEVEL 3: CHALLENGING

107

Suspicious Smoothies

Why do you want to make a smoothie? Who will drink it? Will it be served inside the house or in the backyard? Please answer these questions prior to proceeding. Or don't. And feel free to add any fruit that you like. If you use blackberries, the smoothie will have a somewhat seedy texture.

2 frozen bananas (without peels, of course)
1/2 cup any flavor yogurt (we don't recommend coffee flavor)
Fresh or frozen berries
1 1/4 cup milk and/or juice

Puree all the ingredients in blender. Taste and adjust for sweetness. Add a small amount of honey or sugar if desired, but you probably won't need any sweetener. Serve to whoever, whenever, wherever.

MAKES 1-2

LEVEL 1: EASY

Mysterious Milkshakes

Milkshake-making experiments generally yield delectable results. To make a *Mysterious Vanilla Milkshake,* leave out the chocolate syrup from the second recipe or omit the strawberries from the first recipe.

Strawberry Milkshake

1 cup strawberries, fresh or frozen
1 cup milk
2 teaspoons vanilla
3 ice cubes
1 teaspoon sugar or honey

Combine the ingredients in a blender and puree until smooth. Taste and adjust for sweetness.

MAKES 1-2

Chocolate Milkshake

1-1/2 cups vanilla ice cream
1 cup cold milk
1/3 cup chocolate syrup

Place the ice cream, milk and syrup into a blender. Cover and blend until smooth.

MAKES 1-2

LEVEL 1: EASY

Hot Honey, the Milky Way

This recipe can serve as a sleep-aid. Drink it before bedtime to put yourself in the mood for dreaming.

1 cup milk or plain soy milk
1 tablespoon honey

In the Microwave: Put the honey in the bottom of a ceramic mug. Add half of the milk or soy milk. Microwave for 30 seconds. Stir. Add the rest of the milk.

If the drink isn't hot enough for you, then microwave it again for 10 seconds more. Taste. Add more honey if you like.

On the Stovetop: Put the honey in a pot with the milk or soy milk. Heat over low flame 5 minutes. Test the temperature. Next, taste and adjust for sweetness.

SERVES 1

* The Earth is located within the Milky Way Galaxy which we see as a wide band of light in the night sky.

LEVEL 1: EASY

Fantastic Food Facts

from Earth

Approximately 350 squirts from a cow's udder yield one gallon of milk.

The word "cereal" comes from the name of the Roman goddess Ceres. She was considered the protector of wheat and other grains.

Strawberries are the only fruit that has seeds on the outside.

A ripe cranberry bounces. A spoiled cranberry doesn't.

Corn always has an even number of ears.

For many years in Britain, tomatoes were considered to be poisonous.

Romans shook salt on lettuce and called the new dish *herba salata*, or salted greens. In the USA, we call this "salad."

In ancient Egypt, the onion's round shape and layers symbolized eternity. For this reason, onions were often buried with Pharaohs.

Archaeologists tasted ancient honey that they discovered in an Egyptian tomb. The honey was still edible.

Water freezes at 32 degrees Fahrenheit and boils at 212 degrees Fahrenheit at sea level.

Peanuts are one of the ingredients of dynamite. (More specifically, peanut oil can be processed to produce glycerol, which can then be used to make one of the central ingredients of dynamite.)

Ancient Mayans probably created the first chewing gum when they boiled and chewed the sap of the sapodilla tree.

Bubble gum flavor is actually a combination of wintergreen, vanilla and cassia, a form of cinnamon.

The microwave was invented after a worker walked by a radar tube and his chocolate bar melted in his pocket.

Natural vanilla flavoring comes from a flower called the *orchid*.

One night, an 11 year-old boy left his drink outside. A stirring stick was also in the cup. In the morning, he found his beverage totally frozen. The boy, named Frank Epperson, had invented the first Popsicle!

113

About the Author and Illustrators

When **Ruth Fankushen Kunkel** was eight years old, she imagined that she would own a restaurant one day. Her wish came true when she and her friend Audrey co-created and ran the *Delta of Venus Café* in Davis, California. Later Ruth fulfilled another dream. She helped to create two real boys with her husband Roger. Their older son Gabriel provided all of the initial drawings for *An Alien Robot's Cookbook*.

Gabriel Kunkel now attends the fourth grade in Davis, California. He likes to draw strange creatures and to make traps for his brother Joey and other unsuspecting visitors.

Made in the USA
Charleston, SC
28 January 2011